Aloha Tyson,

Happy Cooking,

Sam Choy's
Cooking with Kids

OTHER BOOKS by
Chef Sam Choy

With Sam Choy
Cooking From The Heart

Sam Choy's Cooking
Island Cuisine At Its Best

The Choy of Seafood
Sam Choy's Pacific Harvest

Sam Choy's Kitchen
Cooking Doesn't Get Any Easier Than This

Sam Choy's Poke
Hawai'i's Soul Food

Sam Choy's Sampler
Welcome to the Wonderful World of Hawai'i's Cuisine

Sam Choy Woks the Wok
Stir-Fry Cooking at its Island Best

Sam Choy's
Cooking with Kids

by
Chef Sam Choy
with **Barbara Burke**

photography by **Douglas Peebles**
edited by **Joannie Dobbs**, Ph.D, C.N.S.

MUTUAL PUBLISHING

Library of Congress Catalog Card
Number: 2001093261

First Printing, October 2001
1 2 3 4 5 6 7 8 9

Art direction by Jane Hopkins and Sistenda Yim
Food styling by Felix Lo
Design by Jane Hopkins
Photos by Ray Wong on the following pages: i, ii, v, xiv, 1, 10
(below), 19 (below), 44 (below), 59 (below), 83 (below),
109 (below).

Softcover
ISBN 1-56647-493-0

Mutual Publishing
1215 Center Street, Suite 210
Honolulu, Hawai'i 96816
Ph: (808) 732-1709
Fax: (808) 734-4094
e-mail: mutual@lava.net
www.mutualpublishing.com

Printed in Korea

Mahalo

A very special Mahalo to these companies whose beautiful art pieces and wares were used in all the recipe photographs. We could not have done it without you. Mahalo ā nui loa.

The Compleat Kitchen

Pier 1 Imports

Chef Sam Choy and his granddaughter
Samantha Pua Mohala Choy

Dear Keiki,

I'm delighted that you want to learn more about cooking. To me, that's what Hawai'i is all about: a love for food and family. When you take time to cook and eat with your family, it confirms that you are all members of the same team, helping and caring about one another.

A lot of kids today have busy schedules. Parents are busy, too. Often, it's hard to find time to prepare a good, home-cooked meal. But, together we can change that.

Spending quality time with family is so important. That's why I wrote this cookbook. I'd like to help inspire you to learn to cook and to eat good meals with your family. Preparing simple dishes—like noodles, beef stew and stir-fry— doesn't have to take a lot of time. I'll show you how to take the chore out of cooking, and replace it with lots of FUN!

Whether you are a beginner or already have some cooking experience, here's a little advice: when it comes to cooking, be bold. Don't be afraid to try something for the first time, whether it is a new food or a new recipe. Instead, say to yourself, "I can do that," or "Sure, I'll try it!"

In the beginning, it's important to learn the basics. Start with some very simple recipes. Cooking is like playing soccer or playing the piano. It takes practice. But I guarantee, the more you cook, the better you will get at it. That's a promise.

Aloha,
Sam Choy

Table of Contents

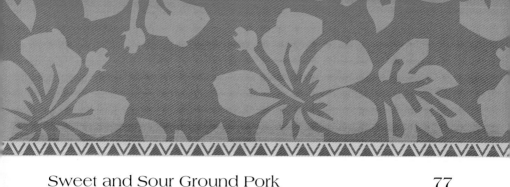

Hints for Parents

Our kids (keiki in Hawaiian) are so special, so precious to us. Making family meals together is a wonderful way to spend quality time with our children and, at the same time, get a wholesome meal on the table. Without inspiring keiki to learn how to cook, preparing home-cooked, family-style dinners may soon become a lost art.

I believe that one consequence of today's fast-food lifestyle is that many young people in Hawai'i have limited food-tasting experiences. They want burgers, chicken or pizza—and reject things that appear different or exotic. This is especially ironic here in the Islands where people once enjoyed great diversity in cuisines.

By exposing kids to cooking in a way that will be both fun and educational, we can provide positive experiences that they will want to repeat over and over again. Here are a few tips:

✔Choose recipes appropriate to the age and cooking experience of your keiki.

✔ Begin by choosing foods that your keiki likes to eat. Gradually expand to new foods and new methods of cooking.

✔ Include your keiki on trips to the grocery store. Teach them how to pick out fruits, vegetables and other food items.

✔ Prepare quantities of food that are reasonable for keiki to handle. Recipes that yield 4 to 6 servings generally work well.

✔ Make accommodations so that keiki can comfortably (and safely) reach range and countertop.

✔ Provide utensils and other equipment that are appropriate to the size of your keiki.

✔ Work together. Keiki learn a lot just by watching. Allow your keiki to develop independent cooking skills at his or her own pace.

Family-Style Cooking

Let me tell you a little about my family and when I was a keiki. I grew up in Lāiʻe on Oahu's North Shore. As a keiki, I first learned about cooking at my dad's lūʻau. For me, that was the fun part of cooking—the lūʻau, barbecues, any kind of cooking outside of the house.

But where I really learned the most about cooking was inside the house. First, I just watched my dad cook. There was something magical about when my dad would turn a whole fish or a whole chicken into a delicious meal.

Soon, my dad let me help him. Our kitchen was like a classroom. My dad took the time to explain so many things to me: the reason why you cook this first, the reason why you use that for flavor, and the reason why you combine certain ingredients together. Spending time with my dad, learning how to cook—it was all so much fun.

My mom was a great teacher, too. I learned so much by going shopping with her. She made sure we were exposed to different kinds of foods. When we went out to eat, Mom always encouraged us kids to try something new.

She also prepared many special holiday meals that are now family traditions.

Today, I have my own family. And, we all love to cook—my wife, Carol, my two sons, even my young granddaughter. We have many great times being together and cooking in the kitchen.

My sons are very different kinds of cooks. Sam Jr., my oldest son, has his own unique cooking style. He's got a mind of his own! Sam is very picky about what he cooks and how he does it. Sam is also adventurous and likes to try lots of new things.

Christopher, my youngest son, is just the opposite. He wants to make sure everything is done the way Grandpa (my dad) taught him. Christopher hates fat! He trims all the fat off before he cooks anything. He enjoys making barbecue and stir-fry dishes.

My little granddaughter, Samantha, is going to be a wonderful chef one day. She's got a great sense of taste. Samantha loves to watch when I cook. I mean, she's really interested! Her favorite dish is saimin. She also likes stews, noodles and rice.

So, just like my mom and dad, I want to share my love of cooking with others. If you learn anything from me, remember this: whenever you cook, make sure it comes from the heart. When you do, just watch. Every meal will turn into a feast!

Before you cook, I hope you will read carefully the following sections. You'll find some important information about food safety, kitchen safety, planning recipes and how to measure ingredients. And, you'll notice that we capitalized all the "Tablespoons" so when you are reading the recipe, there will be less confusion between Tablespoon and teaspoon. Remember—big "T", big spoon; little "t", little spoon. Have fun!

Chef Sam Choy cooks with his granddaughter
Samantha—his favorite little chef.

Food Safety

Germs are all around us. Some are helpful and others harmful. You'll want to protect yourself and your family from harmful germs that can make you sick by learning how to handle food safely. Here are some important steps to follow to help keep food safe.

Buying Food

✔Purchase only the freshest foods.

✔Avoid buying dented cans or food packages that are damaged.

✔Choose fruits and vegetables that are fresh and free of bruises.

✔Ask your parent to help you check dates on meat, fish, poultry and dairy products.

Preparing Food

✔Wash hands.

Germs can get on your hands and under your fingernails. Before cooking, it's important to wash your hands very well, preferably with an anti-bacterial soap. To insure that your hands are really clean, wash them for 20 seconds. This is about the amount of time it takes to sing the "Happy Birthday" song twice.

✔ Wear an apron.

Most people think that you put on an apron to keep your clothes clean. That's true. But more importantly, it's to make sure that none of the germs from your clothes get on the food.

✔ Keep counter, cutting boards, and all cooking equipment clean.

Use hot, soapy water to wash counter and cutting boards. Dry with a clean towel.

✔ Defrost food in the refrigerator.

Try to plan ahead. It may take 1 to 2 days to defrost food in the refrigerator. If you are in a hurry, place the frozen food in a clean sink filled with cold water. Some microwave ovens also have a defrost setting. Follow microwave directions. Avoid defrosting food on the countertop.

✔ Avoid cross contamination.

Raw meat and poultry sometimes contain germs that can make you sick. Luckily, many of these germs are usually killed during cooking. All kitchen items (like knives, bowls, cutting boards) that come in contact with raw meat or poultry should be thoroughly washed with hot, soapy water before using them for other foods.

Serving Food

✔ Germs often multiply at room temperature.

Do not leave perishable foods at room temperature for more than two hours. This includes bentos, musubi, school lunches—also picnic and potluck dishes.

✔Keep hot food hot.

Keep these foods at low heat on the range or in the oven until ready to serve.

✔Keep cold food cold.

Keep perishable food (see Chef Sam's Note) in a refrigerator or in a cooler until ready to use.

Chef Sam's Note

Perishable food: food that need to be stored in the refrigerator or freezer to keep them from spoiling. Examples of perishable food: cheese, hot dogs, an opened jar of mayonnaise.

Non-perishable food: food that may be stored at room temperature, usually in a cool, dark place (like a cupboard) . Examples of nonperishable food: rice, pasta, canned goods.

Kitchen Safety

Most accidents can be avoided. So always be careful when in the kitchen. Take your time. Learn the proper use of kitchen utensils and equipment. Below are some simple safety tips to keep in mind when you are cooking.

Fire

Hopefully, you'll never have a fire in the kitchen. But if you do, here are some fire safety tips:

✔ Call for help. Don't be a hero and try to handle a fire alone.

✔ If something you are cooking in a pan catches on fire, do not panic. It is most likely a grease fire. DO NOT PUT WATER ON IT! Instead, smother the fire by placing a tight-fitting lid on the pan.

✔ If a fire gets out of control and is spreading quickly, warn everyone by yelling, "FIRE." Get everyone out of the house immediately. Then, call 911.

Hair and Clothing

✔ If you have long hair, tie it back or wear a cap when cooking.

✔ Avoid loose clothing, especially long sleeves.

✔ Remove jewelry, such as earrings and rings, as these items can fall into the food.

Major Appliances
Range and Oven

✔ Be careful not to accidentally touch hot burners, or hot oven door or rack.

✔ Avoid placing anything on or near a burner that might catch on fire.

✔ Use pot holders, not dish towels, when moving anything hot.

✔ When cooking on range top, point pot and pan handles from away from the front of the range to prevent them from accidentally being knocked off.

✔ Learn how to set the oven temperature properly.

Microwave Oven

✔ Have an adult show you how to program the microwave before using it.

✔ Never turn on the microwave when the oven is empty inside.

✔ Use only microwave-safe dishes (glass, china, microwaveable plastic). NEVER use metal baking dishes, or plates edged with silver or gold.

Small Appliances

✔ Whenever you use electrical appliances, be careful to keep the cord and appliance away from water.

✔ Make sure the cord does not get in the way of your cooking activities.

✔ Handle all blades carefully.

Blender

✔ Make sure the lid is on tightly before turning on a blender.

✔ Turn off the blender before removing it from the base.

✔ Don't ever place your hand inside the container when the blender is plugged in.

Electric Mixer

✔ Make sure the beaters are inserted properly before turning on an electric mixer.

✔ Turn the mixer off before using a spoon or spatula to scrape ingredients.

Rice Cooker

To avoid getting burned by hot steam, open the rice cooker by lifting the lid AWAY from your body. This is also true when opening any covered pan that contains hot ingredients.

Electric Can Opener

When opening a can, remember that the edges of the lid and can opening will be sharp.

Sharp Utensils

Many kitchen utensils have sharp edges. These include grater/shredders, vegetable peelers and knives. Handle these items carefully. Store them in a safe place.

✔ When using a vegetable peeler, peel in a direction away from your body.

✔When using a grater/shredder, keep your fingers and knuckles away from sharp edges.

✔Select a knife that fits your hand and is a good choice for the task involved.

✔You'll want to learn to use kitchen knives with an adult around to guide you.

✔Remember, A SHARP KNIFE IS SAFER TO USE THAN A DULL ONE. Sharp knives are less likely to slip when chopping or slicing.

✔Keep your fingers, and other people's fingers, away from the knife when in use.

The A B C s
of Cutting

A knife is your best friend in the kitchen. It has so many important uses in cooking.

It's true that knives are dangerous. But you should never be afraid of knives. If you know how to properly hold and use a knife, you should not get hurt. Here are some important tips about knives that you need to know before you begin cooking:

Here are 4 basic kitchen knives:
bread knife
French/chef's knife
table knife
paring knife

A bread knife is serrated, which means its blade has many small, scalloped edges. It is a good choice for cutting soft foods, like bread, tomatoes and cake.

A French knife has a broad blade and a long, sharp edge. It is a chef's favorite choice for cutting vegetables, meats and poultry.

An ordinary table knife is used for spreading and eating at the table. It may also be used to cut soft foods, like bananas and sandwiches.

A paring knife is a small, sharp knife. It is used for peeling, coring and cutting up small amounts of ingredients.

Always pick up a knife by its handle, never by the blade.

Hold the food you are cutting like "a claw." Tuck your fingers underneath your hand. This may seem uncomfortable at first, but you'll get used to it. Take a minute and try it right now. Show me your claw!

When holding food, press hard with your claw so the food does not move. When cutting, the knife should be gently placed against your knuckle. (Remember, fingers tucked underneath!) Take long cuts, away from yourself.

Never cut when your fingers are pointed outward. This is very dangerous!

The RIGHT way to cut   **The WRONG way to cut**

Foods that are round or oddly shaped may move around, and that is very dangerous. Many foods may be cut in half to create a flat surface. Use a chopping board. Do not cut on a countertop or plate.

To chop an onion, carefully slice it in half lengthwise. Peel away the skin. Place one half of the onion flat side down on a chopping board. Hold the onion firmly using your "claw." Carefully cut the onion, holding the slices together. Turn the onion and cut across the slices. They will fall away in chopped pieces.

To pass a knife to someone else, extend the handle to the other person.

When walking while holding a knife, walk with the knife blade facing behind you..

Don't worry about cutting fast right now. That will come with experience. Instead, concentrate on cutting safely.

If a knife falls off the counter, just let it drop. If necessary, jump back a bit to get out of the way. Do not try to catch the knife, or you may get cut.

When you are finished using a sharp knife, set it in a safe place. Never toss it into a sink full of soapy water. You may reach in later and accidently cut yourself.

Before You Cook

By now, you're probably excited to get started cooking. But, hold on! Here are a few more things you'll want to consider before you begin. Take the time to follow these steps, and your recipes should turn out great! You'll find that cooking is as easy as 1-2-3.

1. Read the recipe from start to finish.

Do you understand the directions? Are there any cooking terms that are unfamiliar to you? The glossary in the back of the cookbook describes the cooking terms used in the recipes.

2. Check your ingredients.

Do you have all the necessary ingredients? If not, make a shopping list. Plan your next trip to the grocery store.

3. Determine how much time is needed.

Do you have enough time to complete the recipe? Some recipes, like Fruit Smoothie, can be ready in less than 10 minutes. Other ones, such as Chili Con Carne, need to simmer for up to 3 hours.

When You Are Ready to Cook

1. Assemble your equipment.

✔Preparing a recipe will go faster and easier if you gather everything you need ahead of time.

✔Determine what measuring utensils, mixing bowls, baking dishes, skillets or other equipment you'll need.

✔Organize everything on the counter top before you begin.

2. Get your ingredients ready.

✔See if some ingredients need to be prepared in advance.

✔Gather your nonperishable ingredients on the counter.

✔Keep perishable ingredients in the refrigerator until it is time to use them.

3. Re-read the recipe carefully.

✔Even experienced cooks can make mistakes if they do not take their time reading a recipe.

✔Pay particular attention to the measurements. Does the recipe call for "1 teaspoon" or "1 tablespoon?"

✔Follow the recipe steps in the order given.

Chef Sam's Tip:
Check off ingredients as you add them to a recipe, to make sure nothing is omitted or added twice.

These are the standard measuring utensils you will need:

Dry measuring cups

1/4 cup, 1/3 cup, 1/2 cup and 1 cup

Liquid measuring cups

1-cup, 2-cup, and 4-cup glass measuring cup

Measuring spoons

1/4 teaspoon, 1/2 teaspoon, 1 teaspoon and 1 tablespoon

How to Measure

You may see me prepare a dish on my television show where it appears that I am not measuring ingredients. It may look like I'm preparing a recipe by simply throwing in "some of this" and "some of that." The truth is, through many years of experience, I've learned how to measure ingredients without utensils. But, I do NOT recommend this for a young chef like yourself.

Many recipes, particularly baked goods, require exact measurements. So please, while you are learning to cook, measure everything. Here are some measuring tips to help insure that your recipes are a success.

Dry Ingredients

In general, dry ingredients (like flour and sugar) should be gently scooped into a measuring cup or measuring spoon. Level off any extra ingredient with the straight edge of a table knife or spatula. Below are some of the more common dry ingredients you will measure.

Flour. With a large spoon, gently scoop flour into a measuring cup or spoon. Level off.

Sifted Flour. Scoop flour into a flour sifter. Sift the approximate amount of flour needed into a bowl. With a large spoon, gently scoop sifted flour into a measuring cup or spoon. Level off.

Brown sugar. Scoop brown sugar into a measuring cup or spoon. Press it down to remove any air bubbles. Level off. When firmly packed, brown sugar should hold its shape when emptied from the cup or spoon.

Baking powder, baking soda and spices. Dip the measuring spoon into the container. Level off.

Liquid Ingredients

Measuring large amounts of liquid ingredients:

✔ Always use a clear glass measuring cup for measuring liquid ingredients.

✔ Place glass measuring cup on a level surface.

✔ At eye level, find the line for the amount of liquid you want to measure.

✔Slowly pour the liquid into the measuring cup until it just meets the desired line.

Measuring small amounts of liquid ingredients:

For small amounts of liquid, slowly pour the liquid just to the top of the measuring spoon without letting it spill over. Pour over a small bowl, rather than pouring directly over the ingredients, just in case you pour too much.

Butter and Margarine

✔Use regular butter or margarine in cooking. Only use whipped butter or soft margarine if a recipe specifically says to do so.

✔A 1/4-pound cube of butter or margarine equals 1/2 cup, or 8 tablespoons.

✔For amounts other than 1/2 cup, follow the guidelines on the paper wrapper. Place the cube of butter or margarine on a cutting board. Use a small knife to cut the amount of butter or margarine you need.

More Cooking Tips

Cracking Eggs

✔ Always crack an egg into a separate small bowl, such as a custard cup. This way you can check the freshness and purity of the egg before adding it to the other ingredients.

✔ To crack an egg, tap egg on the side of a bowl. Then using 2 hands, pull the eggshell apart. If necessary, remove any shell which may have fallen into the bowl.

How to Prepare a Baking Pan

Method #1:

Place a small amount of butter, margarine or shortening (about 1 teaspoon) on a baking pan. With a paper towel, spread it all over the surface to evenly coat the pan.

Method #2:

From a distance of about 12 inches, lightly spray vegetable oil to cover baking pan. This will take about 5 seconds of spray. It's a good idea to do this over or near the sink.

Flouring A Pan

Some recipes call for "flouring the pan" after it has been greased. To do this, take a small amount of flour (about 1 to 2 teaspoons) and place it in the pan. Carefully tip the pan from side to side, until the bottom of the pan is lightly dusted with flour. When you have finished, discard any leftover flour.

Some recipes, like muffins and cupcakes, call for paper liners. These can be used in place of greasing the muffin tin.

Breakfast

Breakfast is the most important meal of the day, because it breaks the overnight fast. When you wake up in the morning, your body hasn't eaten for maybe 8 to 10 hours.

Always eat a good breakfast before you start your day at school. You'll be able to focus better, and who knows? Maybe you'll even get better grades if you nourish your body well each morning.

Fruit Smoothie

Fruit Smoothie
Skill Level: Medium

Two favorite island flavors—
banana and pineapple—are combined
together in this delicious fruit smoothie. When
in season, try substituting sliced fresh
strawberries, watermelon, or mango chunks
for the canned crushed pineapple.

Makes 2 servings

Equipment:

measuring cups
measuring spoons
blender

Ingredients:

1 banana
1/2 cup canned crushed pineapple (include heavy syrup)
1 cup milk

1. Peel banana and break into chunks; place into blender.
2. Add pineapple and milk.
3. Press pulse button on blender for a few seconds at a time until blended. Be careful not to over blend or smoothie will become gummy.

Chef Sam's Tip

You can also use frozen bananas to make this drink. To prepare frozen bananas, peel the bananas and place on a jelly-roll pan. Place in the freezer for 30 minutes. Store bananas in a heavy plastic bag or other air-tight container, and freeze until ready to use.

Cinnamon Toast

Cinnamon Toast
Skill Level: Easy

Quick and easy, warm and cinnamon-y—this simple breakfast toast is sure to please.

Makes 8 bite-size pieces

Equipment:
1 small cup or small bowl
measuring spoons
toaster or toaster oven
table knife
optional: fun-shaped cookie cutters

Ingredients:
2 teaspoons cinnamon
2 Tablespoons granulated sugar
2 slices of white or whole wheat bread
2 teaspoons butter or margarine

1. In the cup, mix cinnamon and sugar together until they appear sandy in color.
2. Toast the bread in a toaster (see Tip).
3. While the toast is still hot, butter each piece.

Chef Sam's Tip
If a piece of toast gets stuck in a toaster, **FIRST UNPLUG IT** and then proceed to get the toast out. Chopsticks are a safe and handy utensils for freeing bread from a toaster.

Optional
Try using fun-shaped cookie cutters to cut animal shapes in the toast before serving.

recipe continued on next page

4. Quickly sprinkle the cinnamon-sugar mixture over the buttered toast.

5. Cut the toast from the top left corner to the bottom right corner. Next, without separating the pieces, cut the toast from the top right corner to the bottom of the left corner. Now pull the pieces apart to make four triangles. Repeat with the second piece of sugared toast.

Note: If using a toaster oven, brown both sides of the bread and then follow the above instructions.

Cinnamon Raisin Oatmeal
Skill Level: Easy

There's nothing like a bowl
of home-cooked oatmeal to start off the day.

Makes 2 servings

Equipment:
measuring cups

measuring spoons

medium pot

wooden spoon

Ingredients:
2 cups water

1/2 cup seedless raisins

1 cup minute oatmeal

2 teaspoons cinnamon

2 Tablespoons brown sugar

1. Place water and raisins in a pot and heat until the water starts to boil.

2. Add oatmeal and stir continuously for about 5 minutes to prevent water from boiling over.

3. Remove pot from stove and spoon oatmeal into bowls. (Serve with milk for a creamier-tasting oatmeal.)

4. In a cup, mix cinnamon and brown sugar together until they appear sandy in color. Sprinkle over hot oatmeal.

25

Make-Believe Cornbread
Skill Level: Medium

Here's a cornbread recipe without the cornmeal.
As a result, this recipe is lighter than cornbread, more like a coffee
cake. So, just pretend you're eating cornbread, okay?

Makes 16 pieces

Equipment:
measuring cups

measuring spoons

2 mixing bowls

sifter

whisk or wooden spoon

rubber spatula

8 x 8-inch pan

pot holders

Ingredients:
2 cups reduced-fat Bisquick

3/4 cup granulated sugar

2 teaspoons baking soda

1 cup milk

2 eggs

1/2 pound butter (2 sticks)

vegetable oil spray

1. Let all ingredients reach room temperature.

recipe continued on next page

Make-Believe Cornbread

2. Preheat oven to 350 degrees Fahrenheit.

3. Prepare 8 x 8 inch pan by spraying with vegetable oil spray, such as Pam®.

4. In a mixing bowl, sift Bisquick, sugar, and baking soda. Set aside.

5. In a second mixing bowl, whisk together milk, eggs, and melted butter. Add butter mixture to dry ingredients and mix just until blended.

6. Pour batter into a small 8 x 8 inch pan and bake for 20 to 25 minutes or until golden brown.

7. Cut into squares and serve with jelly or jam.

Chef Sam's Tip

In this recipe, and when preparing other baked goods, DO NOT OVERMIX the batter. Overmixing will result in a tough, rubbery product.

Scrambled Eggs
Skill Level: Easy

The first thing I cooked when
I was 6 years old was scrambled eggs.
And, I burned them. Burnt eggs are stinky!
To avoid making the same mistake I did, pay
close attention to what you are doing.

Makes 2 servings

Equipment:
small bowl

medium bowl

fork

whisk

Teflon frying pan

heat-resistant rubber spatula or wooden
   spoon

pot holders

Ingredients:
4 eggs

2 Tablespoons butter

salt and pepper to taste

1. Crack eggs into a small bowl (see
   directions on page 17)
2. Poke the yolks with a fork. Beat

Chef Sam's Tip
The secret of this recipe is to have the fire at medium heat (not too high). When using a whisk to beat ingredients, the motion is with your wrist—not your arm.

recipe continued on next page

29

with a whisk until it is well blended. Add salt and pepper.

3. Heat frying pan over medium heat. Add butter and continue heating until butter just begins to sizzle. Pour eggs into pan. Immediately begin to stir eggs with a spatula, scraping the pan as you stir. Scrape from the edges of the pan toward the center. Continue scraping until the eggs are set, but still moist.

4. Serve immediately with your favorite bread or rice.

Hard-Cooked Eggs

Skill Level: Easy

Hard-cooked eggs come in their own carrying case (the shell). They are a great breakfast or snack food when you are in a hurry.

Makes 4 eggs

Equipment:

saucepan

pot holders

large slotted spoon

small mixing bowl

Ingredients:

4 eggs

water

1. Place eggs in a saucepan with enough cold water to cover. Bring the water to a boil and then reduce the heat. Simmer over low heat and cook for 15 minutes.

2. Remove pan from heat. Spoon each egg into a bowl of cold water until chilled.

3. With slotted spoon, remove eggs from water. Refrigerate until ready to eat.

Chef Sam's Tip

Chilling the cooked eggs in cold water makes it easier to peel. It also helps to prevent a grayish-green ring from forming around the egg yolks. The ring won't hurt you, but it doesn't look as nice.

Steamed Breakfast Cake
Skill Level: Advanced

Using the dry heat of an oven isn't the
only way to bake. This breakfast cake is prepared
by using steam as a source of heat. If you don't have a wok
for steaming, any large covered pan will do.

Makes 8 pieces

Equipment:
pan with lid or large pan

3 custard cups

measuring cups

mixing bowl

whisk or wooden spoon

rubber spatula

9-inch pie dish

pot holders

Ingredients:
3 cups water

1 egg

1-1/2 cups milk

1/4 cup granulated sugar

2 cups reduced-fat Bisquick®

1. Place custard cups upside down in a pan filled with water.

2. In a mixing bowl, whisk egg, milk and sugar together. Mix in Bisquick® until well blended.

3. Pour mixture into a pie dish. Carefully lower pie dish onto bowls in pan.

4. Cover pan and bring water to a boil. Then reduce the heat to medium and cook cake for about 30 minutes or until a toothpick inserted into cake center comes out clean. REMEMBER TO OPEN THE LID AWAY FROM YOURSELF TO PREVENT FROM BEING BURNED.

5. Serve hot with butter and jelly.

Chef Sam's Tip When preparing baked goods, like cakes or muffins, use large-size eggs unless the recipe tells you otherwise.

Banana-Pineapple Muffins
Skill Level: Advanced

These muffins are so good, that I bet
you won't be able to eat just one. But if you do have
any leftovers, freeze them. Then, when you want a
quick breakfast or snack, pop the frozen muffins
in the microwave for about 30 seconds,
or just long enough to defrost.

Makes 12 muffins

Equipment:

measuring cups

measuring spoons

2 medium mixing bowls

wooden spoon

muffin pan

muffin papers

sifter

pot holders

Ingredients:

1-3/4 cups all-purpose flour

2 teaspoons baking powder

1 teaspoon baking soda

3/4 teaspoon salt

1/4 cup butter (room temperature)

3/4 cup granulated sugar

1 egg

1 teaspoon pure vanilla extract

1/4 cup drained crushed pineapple

3/4 cup mashed ripe bananas

1. Preheat oven to 425 degrees Fahrenheit.

2. In a mixing bowl, sift together flour, baking powder, baking soda, and salt. Set aside.

3. In a second mixing bowl, beat butter until creamy and gradually add sugar. Beat until light and fluffy. Add egg and vanilla and beat well.

4. Add half flour mixture, bananas and pineapple and blend well. Add remaining flour mixture and mix.

5. Place muffin papers into muffin wells and spoon batter into muffin tins. Bake for 20 minutes or until lightly brown.

Cheese Omelet
Skill Level: Advanced

You'll look like a "pro" when you prepare this omelet for your family. There's no limit to the fillings you can use. Try adding diced ham, tomatoes, ripe olives, or green peppers once you've mastered the basic Cheese Omelet recipe.

Makes 1 serving

Equipment:
1 small mixing bowl
measuring spoons
whisk or fork
8-inch non stick skilllet and lid
heat-resistant rubber spatula
grater/shredder
pot holders

Ingredients:
2 eggs
2 Tablespoons water
2 teaspoons cornstarch
1/4 teaspoon salt
1/8 teaspoon black pepper
1 teaspoon butter
3 Tablespoons shredded cheese (divided use)

1. Break eggs into a small bowl. Whisk in water and cornstarch. Season with salt and pepper.

recipe continued on next page

Cheese Omelet

2. In a non-stick skillet, melt the butter over medium-low heat until it begins to bubble. Pour egg mixture into pan and cover to allow steam to cook the omelet.

3. When the egg mixture is nearly cooked, sprinkle 2 Tablespoons cheese on only one-half of the omelet. Then, with the spatula, carefully turn the plain side of the omelet over the cheese side. Slide the omelet onto a plate and sprinkle with remaining shredded cheese.

French Toast
Skill Level: Medium

French toast made with Hawaiian sweet bread is simply heavenly. Serve it with fresh sliced fruit, fruit-flavored yogurt, jam, syrup, or powdered sugar. Your choice!

Makes 6 pieces of toast

Equipment:
large mixing bowl
measuring cups
measuring spoons
whisk or fork
frying pan
pancake turner or spatula
pot holders

Ingredients:
2 eggs
3/4 cup milk
2 teaspoons salt
1 Tablespoon granulated sugar
6 slices Hawaiian sweet bread
2 Tablespoons butter

1. Break eggs into bowl and whisk in milk, salt, and sugar.

recipe continued on next page

39

French Toast

2. Melt butter in frying pan over medium-high heat.

3. Quickly dip bread slices into egg mixture until both sides are coated.

4. Placed coated bread slices onto frying pan. Fry to a light golden color on the bottom of bread and then turn over and brown other side. Repeat with remaining bread slices.

5. Serve hot with your favorite garnish.

Chef Sam's Tip

For fun, use different shaped cookie cutters to make designer French toast.

Puffy Oven Pancake
Skill Level: Medium

If you're not in the mood for pancake flipping, then this is the recipe for you. Simply prepare the pancake batter, pour it in a skillet, and pop it in the oven. Come back half an hour later and you're ready to eat!

Makes 2 servings

Equipment:
I small mixing bowl
measuring cups
measuring spoons
whisk or fork
oven-proof skillet or baking dish
pancake turner or spatula
pot holders

Ingredients:
2 Tablespoons butter
2 eggs
I-1/2 cups milk
I cup flour
I teaspoon salt

Garnish:
Fruit-flavored yogurt, guava jelly or syrup

1. Heat oven to 400 degrees Fahrenheit.

2. Put butter into an oven-proof skillet or baking dish and place into oven just until butter is melted. Remove from oven and, using a paper towel, carefully spread melted butter to grease the bottom of the pan. Set aside.

3. Whisk together the eggs, milk, flour, and salt until a smooth batter is formed. Pour mixture into skillet.

4. Bake for 30 minutes or until puffed and golden brown. While still hot, cut into wedges. Serve with fruit-flavored yogurt, guava jelly or syrup.

Chef Sam's Tip

To make a German Apple Pancake, cut a Golden Delicious apple in half. Peel and core apple, and cut into thin slices. Instead of melting butter in the oven, place skillet on stove over medium-low heat. Add butter and apples and sauté until apples begin to soften. Pour pancake batter over apples and bake in oven for 30 minutes.

Lunch

For busy kids on the go, making lunch needs to be fast and easy. And that's what you'll find in this section—soups and sandwiches that are simple and fun to make.

I've added a new twist to some basic recipes. Toss some frozen vegetables in with your saimin for a colorful and healthy soup. Surprise your friends with a super-duper, triple-decker grilled cheese sandwich. Trade in your "sloppy joe" for a "sloppy dog" with beans. Get ready to have s o m e fun!

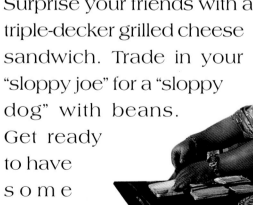

Microwave Tomato Soup

Skill Level: Easy

Here's a different kind of tomato soup that you're sure to like. Using V-8® vegetable juice gives it some extra zing, without being spicy. Serve with saltine or oyster crackers.

Makes 2 servings

Equipment:

2 large glass or ceramic mugs (about 16 fluid ounces each)

measuring cup

pot holders

Ingredients:

I can (12 fluid ounces) V-8® vegetable juice cocktail

I cup milk

1. Pour half of the V-8® juice into each mug.

2. Heat juice in microwave on HIGH for 45 seconds. Stir and heat for an additional 45 seconds. Carefully remove from microwave.

3. Pour half of the milk into each mug and stir once more. Enjoy.

Chef Sam's Tip
Adding cold milk to hot V-8 juice makes the soup the perfect temperature for eating.

45

Vegetable Saimin
Skill Level: Medium

I recommend using fresh saimin in this soup.
It has a firm, chewy texture that makes this dish special.
If fresh saimin is not available, you may use dried
ramen noodles instead. Add your favorite frozen vegetables
for a tasty and colorful meal.

Makes about 3 cups

Equipment:
measuring cup
medium saucepan
pot holders

Ingredients:
1 cup water
1 package fresh saimin or ramen noodles
1 cup diced or sliced frozen mixed vegetables

1. Place water in saucepan and boil over high heat. Add saimin and vegetables and cook until vegetables are tender but firm, about 3 minutes.
2. Pour dry saimin seasoning package into cooked broth and stir.
3. Carefully pour into large soup bowl and serve.

Vegetable Saimin

Basic Grilled Cheese Sandwich
Skill Level: Easy

The secret to making a really good grilled cheese sandwich is choosing the right kind of cheese. Velveeta® is actually a cheese spread but is the classic topping for a Grilled Cheese Sandwich.

Makes I sandwich

Equipment:
bread board
table knife
griddle, electric skillet, or large nonstick frying pan
angle spatula
pot holder

Ingredients:
2 teaspoons butter, room temperature
2 slices sandwich bread
I thick slice of Velveeta® cheese

1. Butter bread on one side only.
2. Heat griddle over medium heat.
3. Place both slices of bread on the griddle, buttered side down. Place a slice of cheese on top of one piece of bread. When the under side of the bread is golden brown, carefully flip the empty slice on top of the bread slice that contains the cheese.
4. With a spatula, remove the sandwich from the griddle and place on bread board. Cut diagonally into triangles.

Triple-Decker
Grilled Cheese Sandwich
Skill Level: Medium

The next time your friends come for lunch
or a sleep-over, surprise them by making this
grilled cheese sandwich.

Makes 1 sandwich

Equipment:
bread board
table knife
griddle
angle spatula
griddle
pot holders
cutting board
paring knife

Ingredients:
3 teaspoons butter (room temperature)
3 slices sandwich bread
2 slices Velveeta® cheese
2 slices ham luncheon meat
1 large slice tomato

1. Butter 3 slices of bread on one
   side only.
2. Heat griddle over medium heat.

recipe continued on next page

49

Triple-Decker Grilled Cheese Sandwich

3. Place slices of bread on the griddle, buttered side down.

4. On the first slice of bread, place 1 slice each of cheese, ham and tomato. On the second slice of bread, place remaining cheese and ham. The third slice of bread is the "lid" for your sandwich, so it remains empty.

5. Layer the sandwich in the order given. With a spatula, remove the sandwich from the griddle and place on bread board. Cut diagonally into triangles.

Tuna Salad Sandwich
Skill Level: Medium

This isn't just an ordinary tuna salad sandwich.
It's got crunchy pieces of celery, shredded cheese,
and just the right amount of lemon juice to
bring out the flavor of the fish.

Makes 2 sandwiches

Equipment:
can opener
measuring cups
measuring spoons
paring knife
cutting board
large bowl
spoon
grater/shredder

Ingredients:
I can (6-1/2 ounces) canned tuna
I cup diced celery
1/2 cup mayonnaise
I Tablespoon lemon juice
1/4 teaspoon salt
1/2 cup shredded cheddar or swiss cheese
4 slices of bread
2 rinsed lettuce leaves
2 slices tomato

1. In a large bowl, combine tuna, celery, mayonnaise, lemon juice, salt, and shredded cheesee and mix.
2. Divide tuna and spread over 2 slices of bread. Top with lettuce and tomato. Place remaining bread on top.
3. Cut sandwiches in half.

Chef Sam's Tip
For variety, use cooked chicken or turkey in place of tuna.

E-Z Cheese Dogs
Skill Level: Easy

There is nothing better than a freshly
cooked hot dog with melted cheese. This recipe makes
it easy (E-Z) to make your own.

Makes 2 sandwiches

Equipment:
bread board
table knife
medium-size pot
tongs
spoon

Ingredients:
2 hot dogs (frankfurters)
water for boiling hot dogs
4 slices of Velveeta® cheese
2 hot dog buns

Condiments:
ketchup, mustard, relish

1. Fill pot half full with water and bring to a rapid
   boil. With tongs, carefully lower hot dogs into
   boiling water. Reduce the heat to medium and
   simmer for about 5 minutes.
2. Meanwhile, open hot dog bun with inside facing

up. Spread your favorite condiments on bun. Top each hot dog bun with 2 slices of cheese.

3. Turn off heat and remove hot dogs with tongs. Place hot dog on top of cheese and close bun. Let hot dog sit for about 30 seconds to allow the cheese to begin to melt.

Sloppy Dogs with Beans
Skill Level: Medium/Advanced

Better not wear your best clothes
when you eat these dogs. They are sloppy,
but oh, so good!

Makes 4 Servings

Equipment:
cutting board
table knife
medium-size pot and cover
spoon
can opener
grater/shredder
pot holder

Ingredients:
1 can (15 ounces) pork and beans
2 Tablespoons brown sugar
2 Tablespoons ketchup
1 teaspoon prepared mustard
4 hot dogs (frankfurters)
4 hot dog buns
1/4 cup shredded Cheddar cheese

1. Place pork and beans into pot and heat over medium heat. Partially cover and heat until small bubbles appear. Add brown sugar, ketchup, and mustard and stir.

Sloppy Dogs with Beans

2. Meanwhile, slice hot dogs into long thin slices. Add to beans and stir. Cook until thoroughly heated (about 5 minutes).

3. Place open buns on plates and top with bean mixture. Sprinkle shredded cheese over top and serve.

Dinner

Hawai'i is a "gathering place" of many cultures. This unique blend of people brings us foods and flavors from all over the world.

In this section, you'll experience Chinese stir-fry chicken, saucy Italian meatballs and my variation of the "good old American" cheeseburger. Get your taste buds ready for a real adventure.

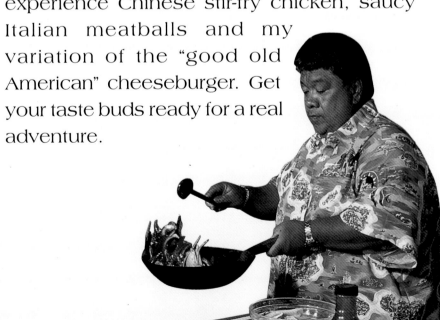

Hamburger Beef Stew
Skill Level: Medium

A classic beef stew can take hours to prepare.
What do you say we speed things up a bit? By using
ground beef instead of chuck roast, you can cut the
cooking time down to less than 30 minutes.

Makes about 10 cups

Equipment:

measuring cups

measuring spoons

mixing bowl

paring knife

cutting board

large stock pot

pot holders

Ingredients:

1 pound lean ground beef

salt and pepper to taste, divided use

flour to dust meat (about 2 Tablespoons)

2 Tablespoons canola oil

3 cups canned beef broth

6 ounces tomato paste

2 cups peeled baby carrots

2 white potatoes

1 medium onion

2 stalks celery

recipe continued on next page

Hamburger Beef Stew

1. Sprinkle ground beef with salt and pepper, then dust with flour. In large pot, heat oil until it begins to sizzle. Carefully add meat to the pot and brown. Cook meat for about 10 minutes on medium, until well browned. Keep stirring to avoid burning.

2. Add beef broth and tomato paste and stir until paste is dissolved in broth. Bring broth to a boil and then reduce heat to maintain a simmer.

3. Cut up carrots, potatoes, onions, and celery into stew size pieces (1-inch cubes). Set aside in separate piles.

4. Add carrots and potatoes and cook 5 minutes. Then add onion and celery and cook 10 minutes more.

5. Add more salt and pepper if necessary.

Chef Sam's Tip

This stew is always better the second day.

Chicken Lū'au Based on My Mother's Favorite Recipe

Skill Level: Medium

My mom taught me how to make Chicken Lū'au. Every year our family has a big Hawaiian lū'au, and this dish is always on the menu.

Makes about 4 cups

Equipment:

measuring spoons

measuring cups

paring knife

cutting board

large wok or skillet

pot holders

Ingredients:

3/4 pound skinless, boneless chicken breast

2 Tablespoons butter

1/2 medium onion, chopped

1 cup chicken stock or low sodium chicken broth

1 cup coconut milk

1 pound rinsed and drained fresh spinach

1/2 teaspoon salt

1. Cut chicken into thin slices. Set aside.

recipe continued on next page

63

Chicken Lū'au Based on
My Mother's Favorite Recipe

2. In a large wok or skillet, heat butter and sauté onions until clear. Add chicken and cook 3 minutes, stirring frequently. Stir-in chicken stock, coconut milk, spinach and salt. Simmer 20 minutes or until chicken is cooked.

3. Serve and enjoy.

Chef Sam's Tip
This Hawaiian dish is traditionally made with young taro leaves, commonly called "lū'au leaf." You can use luau leaf, if available. Otherwise, fresh spinach works just fine.

Saucy Meatballs
Skill Level: Medium

Mama Mia, that's one saucy meatball.
You don't have to be Italian to enjoy this recipe.
Serve these flavorful meatballs over
pasta, rice or French bread.

Makes 16 meatballs

Equipment:
measuring spoons

mixing bowls

large skillet

pot holders

Ingredients:
1 pound lean ground beef

2 slices dry bread, broken into crumbs

1 egg

1 Tablespoon soy sauce or 1-1/2 teaspoons salt

1/8 teaspoon black pepper

1 Tablespoon canola oil

1 can (16 ounces) tomato sauce

2 teaspoons dry Italian herbs or oregano

1. Combine beef, bread, crumbs, egg, soy sauce.
   Sprinkle black pepper over meatball mixture and
   mix.

2. Form 16 meatballs by rolling meat between the palms of your hands until nicely rounded meatballs are formed.

3. Heat oil in large skillet until very hot, but not smoking. Turn down heat and slowly brown meatballs.

4. Pour tomato sauce in skillet and season with herbs. Simmer for about 30 minutes, stirring occasionally to prevent sticking.

5. Serve over pasta, rice, or French bread.

Cooking Pasta
Skill level: Medium

There's a secret to making great pasta.
You want to cook it al dente, which is Italian for
"to the tooth." Cooked pasta should be slightly
chewy when you bite it. Do not overcook
pasta or it will get mushy and fall apart.

Makes varied amount

Equipment:
large pot
pot holders
colander
long-handled spoon

Ingredients:
1 pound dry pasta
water for boiling pasta
oil for pasta pot

1. Fill large pot about 3/4 full with water. Rub a thin layer of oil around inside pot rim to prevent water from boiling over sides.
2. Heat water over high heat to a rapid boil. Carefully pour pasta into hot water; stir. Reduce heat to medium-high and cook pasta until it is *al dente*. Cooking time varies depending upon type of pasta used. Read package directions.

recipe continued on next page

Cooking Pasta

3. Place colander in sink and carefully pour pasta into colander to drain. Even though it may feel awkward, remember to ALWAYS drain hot items by pouring away from your face.

4. Rinse pasta (see Tip below).

5. Top with your favorite homemade or bottled pasta sauce or just some grated cheese.

Chef Sam's Tip

Some recipes call for rinsing pasta and others do not. Rinsing the pasta causes it to wash away the sticky starch and to stop cooking. Not rinsing the pasta causes it to continue cooking a bit and is more sticky.

Chicken Vegetable Stir-Fry

Skill Level: Advanced

Be an artist in the kitchen! By choosing your favorite vegetables, YOU decide the colors and textures of this stir-fry dish. How many colors of the rainbow will you include?

Makes 4 cups

Equipment:

French knife

cutting board

wok or other stir-fry pan

large stirring spoon

Ingredients:

3 cups of your favorite vegetables (such as carrot, celery, zucchini, yellow squash, red onion, red and green bell peppers, shiitake mushrooms)

1 large skinless, boneless chicken breast

2 teaspoons canola oil

1/2 bottle Sam Choy's Stir-Fry Sauce

1/4 cup water

1. Clean and cut the vegetables into pieces of similar size. Set aside.
2. Cut the chicken breast into small strips.

recipe continued on next page

71

Chicken Vegetable Stir-Fry

3. Heat oil in a wok or stir-fry pan over medium-high heat. Once the oil begins to smoke, carefully add chicken and stir lightly until chicken is browned.

4. Add Stir-Fry Sauce to chicken and stir. Cook chicken until almost done, about 2 to 3 minutes.

5. Add vegetables and stir. Add water and cook a few more minutes until the vegetables are crisp-tender.

Chunky Chili Con Carne
Skill Level: Advanced

Did you know that "chili con carne" is
Spanish for "chili with meat?" In Hawai'i, we like our chili
with both meat and beans. Serve it over rice,
with some grated cheese on top.

Makes about 6 cups

Equipment:
sharp knife
cutting board
large skillet or heavy pot
large stirring spoon

Ingredients:
1 pound lean ground beef
1/2 cup chopped onion
1 can (14-1/2 ounces) Hunt®'s whole peeled tomatoes
1 can (8 ounces) tomato sauce
2 Tablespoons chili powder
2 teaspoons minced garlic
1 teaspoon cumin
1/2 teaspoon oregano
1/2 teaspoon salt
1 can (15 ounces) red kidney beans

1. Heat a large skillet over medium-high and brown
   meat with onion.

recipe continued on next page

Chunky Chili Con Carne

2. Stir in tomatoes, tomato sauce, garlic and spices. Simmer for 30 minutes.

3. Add beans and simmer an additional 10 minutes.

Chef Sam's Tip

Kidney beans are commonly used in chili. Other beans work well, too. For variety, try using pinto or black beans.

Sweet and Sour Ground Pork

Skill Level: Medium

Have you ever wondered how
a dish can be both sweet and sour at the
same time? The sweetness comes from the
pineapple, sugar and ketchup. The sour taste
comes from a splash of vinegar.
Add them together and the result
will tickle your taste buds.

Makes about 4 cups

Equipment:
large skillet
large stirring spoon

Ingredients:
I pound ground pork
**Chunky Sweet and Sour Sauce (see recipe
on next page)**

1. In a large skillet, fry ground pork
   over medium heat until no longer
   pink.
2. Add Chunky Sweet and Sour
   Sauce and bring to a simmer,
   then remove from heat.
3. Serve over rice (see recipe on
   page 99)

77

Chunky Sweet and Sour Sauce
Skill Level: Medium

This sweet and sour sauce also
tastes good over chicken and fish.

Makes about 2 cups

Equipment:
measuring spoons

measuring cups

sharp knife

cutting board

saucepan

large skillet

large stirring spoon

Ingredients:
I green bell pepper

2 Tablespoons cornstarch

1/2 cup plus 3 Tablespoons water

1/4 cup white vinegar

3/4 cup granulated sugar

1/4 cup ketchup

I teaspoon peeled and minced fresh ginger

I teaspoon minced fresh garlic

I teaspoon butter

1/3 cup large pineapple chunks

1. Cut top off bell pepper and remove seeds. Dice
   pepper. Set aside.

2. Combine cornstarch with 3 Tablespoons water to make a paste.

3. In a saucepan, combine vinegar, sugar, 1/2 cup water, ketchup, ginger, and garlic. Bring mixture to a boil, stirring to prevent burning. Whisk in cornstarch paste until liquid thickens. Set aside.

4. In a large skillet, heat butter and sauté peppers for 2 minutes. Add pineapple chunks and mix with sweet and sour sauce.

Baked Cheeseburgers

Baked Cheeseburgers

Skill Level: Medium

I bet you've never eaten a cheeseburger like this before. Take a bite and watch the melted cheese ooze out from the center of the patty.

Makes 6 burgers

Equipment:

measuring cup

mixing bowl

6 custard cups

pan that can hold 6 custard cups

table knife

Ingredients:

1 pound lean ground beef

2 cups coarse bread crumbs

1 egg

1/2 cup V-8® vegetable juice cocktail

6 1-inch cubes cheddar cheese

vegetable oil or cooking spray

1. Preheat oven to 350 degrees Fahrenheit.
2. In a medium bowl, mix together ground beef, bread crumbs, egg, and V-8® juice.

recipe continued on next page

3. Spray 6 custard cups with oil. Press half of meat mixture into custard cups filling each 1/2 inch deep. Next, place a Cheddar cheese cube in the center of the cup. Cover with the remaining meat mixture.

4. Place custard cups into pan of hot water and bake for about 45 minutes.

5. Carefully remove pan from oven. Let cool 2 to 3 minutes.

6. Take a knife and cut around the edge of the burger. Turn burgers upside down onto a bun or on top of rice.

Chef Sam's Tip

Always use pot holders, not kitchen towels, when touching hot items.

Sides

With a name like "side dish," you might think this part of the menu is not important. Just the opposite is true. Think about how often you eat a scoop of rice with your meals. Wouldn't your plate seem empty without it?

Side dishes add flavor, color and texture. They make your meal complete. I like to mix and match side dishes. That way, every meal is a surprise!

Sam Choy's Creamy Oriental Dressing
Skill Level: Easy

You're going to love this dressing so much, you won't eat it only on your veggies. You'll also want to spread it on sandwiches and baked potatoes, as well.

Makes about 2/3 cup

Equipment:
measuring spoons
measuring cups
medium-size mixing bowl
whisk

Ingredients:
2/3 cup mayonnaise
4 teaspoons soy sauce
2-1/2 Tablespoons granulated sugar
pinch of white pepper
1 teaspoon black sesame seeds
2/3 teaspoon sesame oil

1. Place all ingredients in a medium-size bowl and whisk together until well blended. If necessary, add in a few drops of water one at a time and whisk until you get the consistency you want.
2. Refrigerate until used.

Tropical Fruit Salad
Skill Level: Medium

One taste of this tropical fruit salad
and you'll know why Hawai'i is called paradise.

Makes about 4 salads

Equipment:
measuring cups
paring knife
melon baller
2 mixing bowls
spoon
4 small salad plates
cutting board

Ingredients:
1 cup canned crushed pineapple
1 cup watermelon balls
1 cup papaya balls
1 banana, sliced
Mānoa lettuce leaves, rinsed and separated
1/4 cup heavy syrup from crushed
   pineapple
1/2 cup plain yogurt

1. Drain crushed pineapple
   reserving 1/4 cup syrup.

recipe continued on next page

Tropical Fruit Salad

2. In a large mixing bowl combine crushed pineapple, watermelon, papaya, and banana. Set aside.

3. Mix together reserved pineapple syrup and yogurt. Pour over combined fruit. Toss gently to coate fruit.

4. Arrange fruit salad in a pretty bowl. If you don't want to use all of the syrup and yogurt mixture, you can serve the remainder in a small cup on the side.

Carrot Raisin Salad
Skill Level: Easy

The combination of carrots and raisins
is a good blend of vegetable and fruit.
Add a few chopped nuts for crunch,
and your mouth will be happy.

Makes about 3 cups

Equipment:
measuring cups
large mixing bowl
vegetable peeler
grater/shredder

Ingredients:
2 large carrots
1/4 cup raisins
1/3 cup mayonnaise

Garnish:
chopped nuts

1. Rinse and peel carrots.
2. Into a large bowl, coarsely grate carrots.
3. Mix with raisins and mayonnaise.
4. Scoop onto plate and top with a sprinkle of nuts.

Carrot Raisin Salad

Macaroni Salad
Skill Level: Medium

In most places, macaroni is thought of as pasta.
In Hawai'i, macaroni is salad. This version adds a little
sweet pickle relish and diced Cheddar cheese. It's good
enough to have two scoops.

Makes about 6 cups

Equipment:

large pot

pot holders

colander

slotted spoon

measuring cups

measuring spoons

paring knife

cutting board

large bowl

Ingredients:

2 cups dry macaroni

water for boiling pasta

oil for pasta pot

I cup diced cheddar cheese

I cup rinsed and chopped celery

1/4 cup sweet pickle relish

I teaspoon salt

2 pinches of black pepper

1. Prepare macaroni (see directions on page 68). Rinse with cold water and drain well.

2. In a large bowl, combine cooked macaroni, Cheddar cheese, celery, and pickle relish. Sprinkle half the salt and black pepper over ingredients; toss. Sprinkle remaining salt and pepper, and toss again.

Somen Noodle Salad
Skill Level: Medium

Somen is a Japanese noodle made from wheat flour.
Don't be fooled. It tastes very different
from Italian-style pasta.

Makes about 6 cups

Equipment:
large pot
colander
pot holders
measuring cups
measuring spoons
paring knife
cutting board
large bowl

Ingredients:

Somen Salad Dressing (see recipe on next page)
1 package (9 ounces) somen noodles
water for boiling pasta
oil for pasta pot
1 wedge iceberg lettuce (about 1/4 head)
1 cup thinly sliced ham
1 hard boiled egg, diced
1 small cucumber, cut into thin strips

1. Prepare Somen Salad Dressing.

recipe continued on next page

92

Somen Salad

2. Cook somen noddles (see directions on page 68). Rinse with cold water and drain well.

3. Shred lettuce.

4. In a large bowl combine cooked somen, lettuce, ham, egg, and cucumber.

5. Toss with Somen Salad Dressing and serve.

Somen Salad Dressing

Skill Level: Easy

Kids love this dressing because it is sweet and nutty tasting.

Makes about 3/4 cup

Equipment:
measuring spoons
medium bowl

Ingredients:
3 Tablespoons rice vinegar

2 teaspoons vegetable oil

2 teaspoons toasted sesame oil

3 Tablespoons soy sauce

2 Tablespoons granulated sugar

I Tablespoon sesame seeds

1. Combine ingredients and whisk together.

94

Potato Salad
Skill Level: Medium

It's hard to decide which salad is more popular in Hawai'i, macaroni salad or potato salad. Try them both and pick your favorite.

Makes about 3 cups

Equipment:
large saucepan
pot holders
vegetable brush
paring knife
colander
large mixing bowl
wooden spoon
measuring cup

Ingredients:
4 red potatoes (about 2 cups)
2 hard-cooked eggs, diced
I cup chopped celery
1/2 cup mayonnaise or Sam Choy's Creamy Oriental Dressing
1/4 cup minced mild-flavored onion (red or 'Ewa)

1. Scrub potatoes with brush and remove any blemishes or

recipe continued on next page

95

sprouts. Cut potatoes, if necessary, to insure that they are the same size and will cook evenly.

2. Rinse and place potatoes in saucepan with enough cold water to cover. Bring the water to a boil. Then reduce the heat and simmer until just tender, about 10 to 15 minutes.

3. Drain potatoes away from face into a colander. Set aside in a large mixing bowl until cool. Remove peel if desired and then cut into bite-size pieces.

4. When potatoes are cool, add other ingredients and toss.

Basic White or Brown Rice—Rice Cooker Method

Skill Level: Easy

Okay, you found it. These are the easiest recipes in the whole cookbook.

Makes about 3 cups

Equipment:
measuring cups
rice cooker
rice paddle to serve
pot holders
fork

Ingredients Proportions:

white long-grain rice:
   I cup rice to I cup water
white medium-grain rice:
   I cup rice to I cup water
brown rice:
   I cup rice to 2 cups water

1. Combine rice and water. Cover and press "Cook" button. Cooking will take 30 to 40 minutes.
2. When cooked, fluff rice with a fork.
3. Cover with a lid and allow to sit for 5 minutes before serving.

Basic White or Brown Rice Stove-top Method
Skill Level: Easy

Makes about 3 cups

Equipment:
measuring cups
2-quart saucepan and lid
rice paddle to serve
pot holders
spoon

Ingredients Proportions:
white long-grain rice:
　I cup rice to 1-1/4 cups water
white medium-grain rice:
　I cup rice to 1-1/2 cups water
brown rice:
　I cup rice to 2-1/4 cups water

1. In a 2-quart saucepan, bring water to a boil. Add rice. Over very low heat, cover and cook until water is absorbed (about 15 minutes).
2. Remove from heat and stir once. Replace cover and let stand for 5 to 10 minutes before serving.

Basic White or Brown Rice Microwave Method

Skill Level: Easy

Makes about 3 cups

Equipment:
measuring cups
1-1/2 quart glass casserole dish and cover
rice paddle
pot holders

Ingredients Proportions:
white long-grain rice:
I cup rice to 1-3/4 to 2 cups water
white medium-grain rice:
I cup rice to 1-1/2 to 1-3/4 cups water
brown rice:
I cup rice to 2-1/2 cups water

1. Add rice and water to a 1-1/2 quart glass casserole dish, cover.
2. Heat on high for 5 minutes; medium for 15 minutes.
3. Remove from microwave and let sit with cover on for 5 minutes before serving.

Fried Rice
Skill Level: Medium

Now, here's a recipe that lets you get really creative.
Start with my basic recipe for Fried Rice. If you don't have
lup cheong (Chinese pork sausage), substitute Portuguese
sausage, bacon, Spam or fishcake instead. You can even change
the vegetables, if you like. When you're done, rename the dish
"_____'s Fried Rice" (insert YOUR name in the blank).

Makes about 3 cups

Equipment:
measuring cups

measuring spoons

large skillet

wooden spoon

paring knife

cutting board

pot holders

Ingredients:
2 lup cheong sausages (Chinese pork sausage)

2 Tablespoons peanut oil

1/4 cup diced onion

2 Tablespoons diced green pepper

1 can (5 ounces) sliced water chestnuts, drained

1 hard cooked egg, diced (see recipe on page 31)

2 Tablespoons soy sauce

1 teaspoon granulated sugar

recipe continued on next page

Fried Rice

1 teaspoon peeled and minced ginger or 1/2 teaspoon ground ginger

2 cups cooked rice

1. Dice lup cheong.

2. Heat peanut oil in a large skillet and add lup cheong. Stir-fry for 5 minutes to assure sausage is fully cooked.

3. Add onion and green pepper. Stir-fry until the onion is nearly translucent.

4. Add water chestnuts, egg, soy sauce, sugar, ginger, and rice to skillet. Stir-fry over low heat for about 10 minutes.

Chef Sam's Tip

This recipe works best when you use leftover rice that has been chilled for several hours.

Mashed Potatoes
Skill Level: Medium

Mash them. Bash them. All that matters is that you smash them. Mashed potatoes taste good with just about everything. So, serve them as a side dish at any meal.

Makes about 4 cups

Equipment:
measuring spoons

saucepan

colander

mixing bowl

pot holders

potato masher or fork

Ingredients:
1 pound potatoes (about 3 medium)

4 to 8 Tablespoons milk

2 Tablespoons soft butter

1/2 teaspoon salt

dash of pepper

1. Peel potatoes and cut into 1-inch slices. Rinse well and place potatoes in saucepan with enough cold water to cover.
2. Place pan over medium-high

recipe continued on next page

heat. Bring water to a boil. Reduce heat and simmer uncovered, until just tender, about 15 minutes.

3. Drain potatoes in colander, making sure you pour away from your face. Gently shake colander to remove excess water.

4. Turn potatoes into a large mixing bowl. Mash potatoes until no lumps remain.

5. Add 2 Tablespoons of milk and beat. Repeat until the potatoes are smooth and fluffy. Do not overbeat potatoes or they will become gummy.

6. Stir in butter, salt and pepper.

Chef Sam's Tip

To peel or not to peel? If you want really smooth, creamy mashed potatoes, you'll need to peel the potatoes. In a hurry? Scrub your potatoes well and boil them with the skins on. Then mash them— skins and all. Either way, they'll taste terrific.

Oven-Baked French Fries

Skill Level: Advanced

Oven baked French fries taste somewhere between a French fry and a baked potato. Dip them in ketchup or shoyu. They are so delicious!

Makes about 3 cups

Equipment:

measuring spoons

vegetable peeler

paring knife or French knife

cutting board

baking pan

pot holders

ruler

angle spatula

Ingredients:

4 baking potatoes

butter-flavored vegetable oil spray

1/4 teaspoon salt, divided in half

1. Preheat oven to 450 degrees Fahrenheit.
2. Peel potatoes. First cut them in

recipe continued on next page

Oven-Baked French Fries

half lengthwise and then cut them into lengthwise strips 1/2-inch wide by 3/8-inch thick.

3. Rinse them with water and quickly dry them with a paper towel.

4. Arrange strips in a baking pan so that they do not touch.

5. From about 12 inches away, spray potatoes with vegetable oil spray for about 5 seconds. Sprinkle with half of the salt.

6. Flip potatoes and spray other side. Sprinkle with remaining salt.

7. Bake for 15 minutes. Using pot holders, remove pan from oven. Use a spatula to flip potatoes over and separate them. Return to oven for an additional 15 minutes.

8. Carefully remove from oven and slide fries onto a platter.

Chef Sam's Tip

Season these potatoes with Italian herbs and you have "pizza fries." Sprinkle them with furikake and you have "local fries." Give them a try!

Steamed Vegetables
Skill Level: Medium

Steaming is a great way to cook vegetables.
Wait until you see how brightly colored the vegetables become.

Makes 4 servings

Equipment:
large pot with lid
steamer basket
fork
pot holders

Ingredients:
4 cups of your favorite vegetables

1. Wash vegetables.
2. Peel vegetables that need peeling (carrots, potatoes, etc.).
3. Cut vegetables into pieces of the same size.
4. Fill pot with 3 inches of water. Open steamer basket and set inside pot.
5. Evenly distribute vegetables in steamer basket.
6. Bring water to a boil. Cover. Reduce heat and simmer 10 to 15 minutes, or until vegetables are crisp-tender. When removing lid, remember to open the lid away from your face.

Chef Sam's Tip
Steamed vegetables taste good just as they are. These veggies also taste good sprinkled with sesame seeds. Still another idea is to serve them with a bottled salad dressing or dipping sauce.

Snacks & Sweets

Hawai'i's tropical fruits give us so many delicious flavors. Hawai'i has the best desserts and snacks in the world. Yes, I'm biased. But it's true. So, I hope you have as much fun making them as you will enjoy eating them.

For a special occasion, layer squares of haupia and fresh fruit in a parfait glass. If you like chocolate, get ready for my killer brownies or double-chocolate chip cookies.

Homemade Hurricane Popcorn
Skill Level: Easy

Two local ingredients—furikake and
arare rice crackers—change ordinary popcorn
into a mouth-watering snack. Watch out,
Mom! We're going to make a
hurricane in the kitchen.

Makes about 5 cups

Equipment:
measuring cups

measuring spoons

microwave or popcorn maker

brown paper bag

Ingredients:
5 cups popped popcorn (see Chef Sam's Tip)

5 sprays of butter-flavored vegetable oil spray

1 Tablespoon furikake

1/2 teaspoon granulated sugar

1/4 cup arare rice crackers

salt to taste

1. Place popped popcorn in a clean brown paper
   bag and spray popcorn inside bag with
   vegetable oil spray.
2. Sprinkle furikake and sugar onto popcorn and
   add arare rice crackers to bag. Fold bag closed,

hold tight and shake to evenly distribute the ingredients.

3. Pour into a bowl and enjoy.

Chef Sam's Tip
Use microwaved popcorn or place 2 Tablespoons unpopped popcorn into a hot air popcorn maker. Will 2 Tablespoons of unpopped popcorn yield 5 cups popped? Wow!

Boiled Fresh Peanuts
Skill Level: Easy

A little salty, a little sweet—
these peanuts are a real treat.

Makes about 2 cups

Equipment:
measuring cups

measuring spoons

large pot with lid

colander

pot holders

Ingredients:
I pound raw peanuts

I/4 cup coarse sea salt

4 star anise

I teaspoon granulated sugar

1. Place peanuts into pot and cover with water. Add salt, star anise and sugar.

2. Place pot on burner and heat until the water reaches a boil (big bubbles). Cover the pot with the lid and lower the heat so that the water just simmers (tiny bubbles). Simmer for about 1-1/2 hours.

3. Remove pan from stove and drain peanuts away from face and into a colander. Cool and refrigerate before serving.

Double Chocolate Chip Cookies

Skill Level: Medium

When regular chocolate chip cookies aren't chocolate-y enough, try these "double chocolate" delights. Cocoa powder is your secret ingredient in this delicious cookie recipe.

Makes about 36 cookies

Equipment:

measuring cups

measuring spoons

table knife or flat spatula

mixing bowl

wooden spoon

sifter

jelly-roll pan or cookie sheet pan

2 teaspoons for dropping cookies

pot holders

plate

Ingredients:

1-1/4 cups room temperature butter

2 cups granulated sugar

2 eggs

1 teaspoon pure vanilla extract

2 cups all-purpose flour

recipe continued on next page

Double Chocolate Chip Cookies

1-1/4 cups unsweetened cocoa powder

1 teaspoon baking soda

2 cups semi-sweet chocolate chips

1. Preheat oven to 350 degrees Fahrenheit.
2. In a bowl, cream butter and sugar with a wooden spoon until light and fluffy. Add eggs and vanilla extract until just combined.
3. In a separate bowl, sift together flour, cocoa powder, and baking soda. Add dry ingredients to creamed mixture. Stir in chocolate chips. Mix until combined. Chill dough for one hour.
4. Drop by teaspoonful onto ungreased jelly-roll pan and bake for 8 to 10 minutes. Cool for 5 minutes on a plate.

Chef Sam's Tip

For chewier cookies, lower the oven temperature to 325 degrees Fahrenheit and increase baking time by about 5 to 10 minutes.

Corn Flake Coconut Macaroons
Skill Level: Easy

You don't need to climb a tree
for this coco-nutty treat. Keep a batch of these crisp,
chewy coconut cookies on hand for a quick,
after school snack.

Makes about 30 cookies

Equipment:
measuring cups

measuring spoons

mixing bowl

wooden spoon

jelly-roll pan or cookie baking sheet

2 teaspoons

pot holders

Ingredients:
1/4 cup shortening

3/4 cup granulated sugar

1 large egg

1/2 cup finely chopped almonds

1/2 cup shredded coconut

1/4 teaspoon almond extract

5 cups corn flakes

1. Preheat oven to 350 degrees Fahrenheit.

2. Lightly grease jelly roll pan or cookie baking sheet.

3. In a large bowl, blend shortening and sugar; add egg and beat well. Mix in nuts, coconut, and almond extract. Then stir in corn flakes.

4. Drop by teaspoons onto baking sheet. Bake for 12 to 15 minutes. Watch cookies closely so they do not burn.

5. Let cookies cool slightly before removing from jelly-roll pan.

Chef Sam's Tip

Sam's Killer Candy Brownies

Sam's Killer Candy Brownies

Skill Level: Medium

If you love chocolate, then this recipe is for you. Before baking, the brownie batter is sprinkled with either chocolate chips or bits of your favorite chocolate candy.

Makes 16 brownies

Equipment:

measuring cups

measuring spoons

mixing bowl

wooden spoon

sifter

8 x 8-inch pan

wire rack

pot holders

Ingredients:

1 cup butter, at room temperature

1 cup brown sugar

1 cup granulated sugar

4 eggs

1 teaspoon vanilla

1-1/2 cups all-purpose flour

1/2 cup unsweetened cocoa powder

1 teaspoon baking powder

recipe continued on next page

1/2 teaspoon salt
1 cup chocolate chips or chocolate candy pieces

1. Preheat oven to 350 degrees Fahrenheit.
2. Grease pan with butter.
3. In a large mixing bowl, beat together butter, brown sugar and granulated sugar. Beat in eggs and vanilla.
4. In a separate bowl, sift the flour, cocoa, baking powder and salt. Add to the creamed mixture. Mix until combined well.
5. Pour the brownie batter into pan and sprinkle chocolate chips or candy of your choice on top. Bake for 30 minutes.
6. Cool on wire rack. Slice into 2 x 2-inch pieces when cool.

Pineapple Macadamia Nut Bread

Skill Level: Medium/Advanced

Two of Hawaii's favorite foods—
pineapple and macadamia nuts—are used
in making this delicious bread. Eat it
for breakfast or as a snack.

Makes 1 loaf

Equipment:

measuring cups

measuring spoons

mixing bowl

wooden spoon

sifter

9 x 5 x 3-inch loaf pan

pot holders

wire cooling rack

Ingredients:

2 cups sifted flour

1/2 cup granulated sugar

2 teaspoons baking powder

1/4 teaspoon baking soda

1 teaspoon salt

1/2 cup chopped macadamia nuts

2/3 cup all-bran cereal

recipe continued on next page

Pineapple Macadamia Nut Bread

2/3 cup pineapple syrup, drained from canned fruit

2/3 cup well-drained crushed pineapple

I large egg, well beaten

2 Tablespoons butter (room temperature)

1. Preheat oven to 300 degrees Fahrenheit.

2. Grease and flour loaf pan; set aside.

3. In a large bowl, sift together first five ingredients. Stir in macadamia nuts and set aside.

4. In a medium-size bowl, combine cereal, pineapple syrup, and crushed pineapple. Let mixture stand 20 minutes and then add egg and butter. Add this mixture to flour mixture stir until blended. Pour into prepared loaf pan.

5. Bake for 60 to 75 minutes or until toothpick inserted into center of loaf comes out clean.

Chef Sam's Tip

Coconut Bread Pudding
Skill Level: Advanced

It's rich and creamy, loaded with coconut and
macadamia nuts. It's not a pie. It's not a cake.
What kind of dessert is it?
(Answer: See recipe below)

Makes 8 servings

Equipment:
measuring cups

measuring spoons

mixing bowl

whisk

rubber spatula

medium casserole or baking dish

shallow pan (larger than casserole or baking dish)

pot holders

Ingredients:
3 eggs

3/4 cup granulated sugar

4 cups milk

6 Tablespoons coconut milk

8 cups diced French bread

1/2 cup chopped macadamia nuts

1/2 cup shredded coconut

1. Preheat oven to 325 degrees Fahrenheit.

recipe continued on next page

124

Coconut Bread Pudding

2. Spray baking dish with a light coating of oil.

3. Whisk eggs and sugar together. Add milk and coconut milk, and mix thoroughly to make a custard. Set aside.

4. Layer bread, macadamia nuts, and coconut flakes in casserole dish. Pour custard mixture evenly over top, letting it soak into bread.

5. Place medium casserole into shallow baking pan. Pour sweet bread mixture into casserole dish. Half-fill shallow pan with hot tap water.

6. Bake for about 1 hour or until a knife inserted in the center comes out clean. Serve warm or cold.

Chef Sam's Tip

Garnish with coconut syrup, diced pineapple, or sliced strawberries.

Too Cool Fruit Dessert
Skill Level: Medium

▲▽▲▽▲▽▲▽▲▽▲▽▲▽▲▽▲▽▲▽▲▽▲▽▲▽▲▽▲▽▲▽▲▽▲▽

Choose your favorite fruit, fresh or canned,
to make this cool summer dessert. It's easy!
Just layer squares of haupia with colorful,
diced fruit in a glass dish.

Makes 4 servings

Equipment:

measuring cups

cutting board

knife

4 glass dishes

Ingredients:

**I recipe Haupia Squares (see recipe on
page 129)**

2 cups diced fresh or canned fruit

mint sprigs (optional)

1. Cut haupia into small squares.
2. Layer each glass with haupia
   and diced fruit. Top with a mint
   sprig (optional).

Too Cool Fruit Dessert

Haupia Squares
Skill Level: Medium

⟨⟨⟨⟨⟨⟨⟨⟨⟨⟨⟨⟨⟨⟨⟨⟨⟨⟨⟨⟨⟨⟨⟨⟨⟨⟨⟨⟨⟨⟩

Haupia is a chilled coconut dessert served at
lūraus. I bet you can't eat just one of these
heavenly haupia squares.

Makes 6 servings

Equipment:

measuring cups

measuring spoons

mixing bowl

rubber spatula

8 x 8-inch pan

medium saucepan

pot holders

spoon

Ingredients:

1/2 cup granulated sugar

1/4 cup cornstarch

I can (12 ounces) frozen coconut milk

I cup whole milk

1/2 cup sweetened shredded coconut
  flakes, divided in half

1. In a mixing bowl, stir together
   sugar and cornstarch. Add

recipe continued on next page

coconut milk and whole milk and stir to blend. Pour mixture into a saucepan.

2. Over medium heat, cook until the mixture bubbles and thickens. Remember to stir frequently to prevent the mixture from burning or becoming lumpy.

3. Stir half the coconut into haupia mixture.

4. Pour mixture into pan and place in the refrigerator until well-chilled.

5. Garnish with remaining coconut. Cut into squares and serve.

Mango Cobbler

Skill Level: Medium

A cobbler is a topsy-turvy,
"upside down" pie. Why? Because a
cobbler's crust is found on the top of
the dessert, not on the bottom.

Makes 12 pieces

Equipment:

measuring cups

measuring spoons

2 mixing bowls

whisk

wooden spoon

9 x 13 x 2-inch baking dish

pot holders

Ingredients:

1 cup granulated sugar

1 cup butter, room temperature

2-3/4 cups all-purpose flour

3 Tablespoons brown sugar

2 Tablespoons all-purpose flour

1 Tablespoon cinnamon

6 cups diced mangoes

vegetable oil cooking spray

1. Preheat oven to 350 degrees
   Fahrenheit.

recipe continued on next page

131

2. Spray baking dish with a light coating of oil.

3. In a mixing bowl, whisk together granulated sugar and butter until creamy. Then sprinkle flour slowly over butter mixture and combine until slightly crumbly and moistened. Be careful not to overmix.

4. In a cup, stir together brown sugar, 2 Tablespoons flour and cinnamon.

5. In a second bowl, place diced mangoes and sprinkle brown sugar mixture over fruit until coated evenly. Spoon mangoes into prepared 9 x 13 x 2 baking dish.

6. Sprinkle cobbler crust (sugar, flour and butter mixture) over the top of mango. Bake for 30 minutes or until the crust turns a golden brown.

Chef Sam's Tip

This recipe melts in your mouth. Serve plain, with whipped topping or ice cream.

Roasted Apple Bananas
Skill Level: Easy

There is something unique
and special about the flavor of apple bananas.
This fruit has the texture of a banana,
but the flavor of an apple. Try it and
see for yourself.

Makes 4 servings

Equipment:

glass cup

measuring spoons

mixing bowl

paring knife

teaspoon

pastry brush

8 x 8-inch baking pan

pot holders

Ingredients:

4 apple bananas

4 teaspoons butter, room temperature

2 teaspoons fresh lemon juice

2 teaspoons granulated sugar

vegetable oil spray

1. Preheat oven to 375 degrees
   Fahrenheit.

recipe continued on next page

2. Prepare baking pan by spraying with vegetable oil spray.

3. Roll lemon on table until you feel that it is getting soft. Cut the lemon in half and squeeze. Remember to remove seeds with a strainer or spoon.

4. Place butter in a small dish, cover, and microwave for about 10 seconds, or until just melted. Mix melted butter with fresh lemon juice.

5. Peel bananas and place in prepared baking pan.

6. Brush banana with butter-lemon mixture and sprinkle with sugar.

7. Bake for about 15 minutes, or until tender.

Chef Sam's Tip

A pastry brush is a special brush that is used exclusively for cooking. If you don't have a pastry brush, use a spoon to drizzle the lemon-butter mixture over bananas.

Banana-Melon Split with Creamy Honey-Lime Sauce

Skill Level: Medium

*This is one of my favorite recipes—
fresh fruit topped with a honey-lime sauce.
It's so refreshing on a hot summer day. Make it
for your family or as a party dessert.*

Serves 4

Equipment:

measuring cups

measuring spoons

melon ball cutter

paring knife

cutting board

ice cream scoop

banana split bowl or any fun bowl

Ingredients:

1 cup cottage cheese

1/2 teaspoon fresh lime juice

2 Tablespoons honey

1/2 cup frozen raspberries

1/2 cup orange juice

2 apple bananas, peeled and sliced
   lengthwise

recipe continued on next page

135

Banana-Melon Split
with Creamy Honey-Lime Sauce

8 ice cream scoops watermelon

4 melon baller scoops canteloupe

I cup crushed pineapple

1/4 cup chopped nuts

4 red flame seedless grapes

1. Combine cottage cheese, lime juice, honey, raspberries, and orange juice in a blender. Pulse blend until smooth. Set aside.

2. In 4 banana split bowls, arrange bananas, watermelon, and canteloupe. Pour honey dressing over fruit and top with crushed pineapple, chopped nuts, and a single red flame grape.

The "Big Banana" Split
Skill Level: Easy

This banana split is like none you have ever eaten before.
It has bananas, ice cream, fresh fruit, chocolate candy and
li hing mui gummy bears. All I can say is, "Wow!"

Makes 4 servings

Equipment:
measuring cups

measuring spoons

knife

4 large ice cream bowls

ice cream scoop or large spoon

Ingredients:
2 large ripe bananas

4 large scoops of vanilla ice cream

1 cup diced fresh mango

8 fresh raspberries

1 chocolate candy bar of your choice, broken into pieces

16 li hing mui gummy bears

1. Place out 4 large ice cream bowls.
2. Peel bananas and slice in half lengthwise.
3. Start building banana splits in bowls by layering banana topped with ice cream. Add mango and raspberries. Top with chocolate candy pieces and gummy bears.

The "Big Banana" Split

Li Hing Mui Ice Cakes
Skill Level: Easy

▲▽▲▽▲▽▲▽▲▽▲▽▲▽▲▽▲▽▲▽▲▽▲▽▲▽▲▽▲▽
"Ice cake" isn't really a cake at all.
It's a fruit-based frozen dessert. This recipe is
flavored with li hing mui powder.

Makes 8 cups

Equipment:
measuring cups
measuring spoons
mixing bowl
wooden spoon
8 (3-ounce) paper baking cups
8 x 8-inch pan
chopstick

Ingredients:
1 cup orange soda
1 cup water
2 Tablespoons li hing mui powder (see Tip)
6 Tablespoons granulated sugar
1 Tablespoon fresh lemon juice

1. Thoroughly mix all ingredients together.
2. Place cups in an 8 x 8-inch baking pan for ease of handling.

Li Hing Mui Ice Cakes

3. Fill paper cups about two-thirds full to ensure that they don't overflow during freezing.

4. Place in freezer for about 1-1/2 hours. Remove from freezer, stir each cup with chopstick, and return to freezer until hard.

Chef Sam's Tip

Put less li hing mui powder for a sweeter taste or more for a sharper taste. There is no substitute for li hing mui powder.

Kids Can Cook Edible Fishbowl

Skill Level: Easy/Medium

Here's a fun party dish that you can
make in a real aquarium. Simply create a sea
of blueberry gelatin and fill with a school
of candy "gummy fish."

Serves 20 to 32

All proportions are up to you but here are some suggestions:

I clean glass aquarium bowl or a large glass bowl

6 packages (3 ounces each) blueberry gelatin

4 cups seedless white grapes, stems removed

Gummy fish candy (how many fish is strictly up to you and your aquarium size)

1. Clean aquarium first with soap and water, then with bleach and cold water. Rinse with lots of water. Use a clean dish towel to dry or drain upside down.

2. Scatter grapes in bottom of aquarium or bowl.

3. Make gelatin according to package directions and pour into aquarium or bowl. When gelatin is halfway set, sink gummy fish into gelatin and let firm.

Chef Sam's Note

You can add all types of gummy critters to personalize your aquarium.

Kids Can Cook Edible Fishbowl

Index

Notes

Notes

_____

_____

_____

_____

_____

_____

_____

_____

_____

_____

_____

_____

_____

_____

_____

_____